Jib Trimming

An Illustrated Guide

Felix Marks

Jib Trimming

An Illustrated Guide

Felix Marks

With Photography by Neil Hinds

www.fernhurstbooks.co.uk

First published 2005 by
Fernhurst Books
Duke's Path
High Street
Arundel
West Sussex BN18 9AJ
United Kingdom

Phone: +44 (0) 1903 882277
Fax: +44 (0) 1903 882715
Email: sales@fernhurstbooks.co.uk
Web: www.fernhurstbooks.co.uk

ISBN 1 904475 22 1

British Library Cataloguing in Publication Data:
A catalogue record for this book is available from the British Library

Cover design by Felix Marks
Photographs by Neil Hinds
Illustrations by Felix Marks

Acknowledgements
The Author gratefully acknowledges the help of Neil Hinds for all photography. Ian
MacDiarmid, Melissa Collins, Anna Waddington, Martin White, Lucy McInnes,
Conrad Johnston, Katrina Aked, and Lynn Marks and are also thanked for their help
in developing this book.

Contents

FOREWORD 7

SECTION 1 CREATING LIFT AND AVOIDING DRAG 8

    CREATING LIFT WITH AIRFOILS 9
    AIRFOIL: AIRPLANE WING 10
    AIRFOIL: SAIL 11
    AVOIDING DRAG WITH AIRFOILS 12

SECTION 2 THE JIB AND ITS CONTROLS 13

    ANNOTATED PICTURE OF JIB 14
    JIBS AND GENOAS 15
    WINCHES 16
    CLEATS 17
    CLAM CLEAT VS. SELF-TAILING WINCH 18
    HOISTING THE JIB 19

SECTION 3 SAIL SHAPE 20

    OVERALL JIB TRIMMING GOALS AND MEANS 21
    SAIL SHAPE: BELLY (DEPTH) 23
    SAIL SHAPE: GROOVE 26
    SAIL SHAPE: FOOT 31
    SAIL SHAPE: LEECH (TWIST) 34
    THE COMPLETE SHAPES 37
    READING THE TELLTALES 40

SECTION 4 EVERYTHING CHANGES ALL OF THE TIME 42

    EVERYTHING CHANGES ALL OF THE TIME 43
    TACKING 44
    BACKING THE JIB 45
    USING GEARS 46
    FOOTING 50
    WIND CHANGES 52
    SEA STATE 54

SECTION 5 OFFWIND TRIM 55

    OFFWIND TRIM: REACHING 56
    DOWNWIND TRIM: RUNNING 59

CONCLUSION 62

APPENDIX A - SETTING UP...**63**

    SPREADER MARKS 64

    JIB TRACK 65

    GENOA TRACK 67

    JIB HALYARD 68

APPENDIX B - TRIM TABLE TEMPLATE......................................**69**

    TRIM TABLE TEMPLATE...70

APPENDIX C - POINTS OF SAIL..**71**

GLOSSARY...**72**

INDEX..**77**

Foreword

So you want to be a jib trimmer …

Jib trimming is one of the most prized roles on a boat. It requires a deep and subtle appreciation of sail shapes and the controls used to achieve them. This book is here to help and has been written in a ground breaking way. The approach we have taken is to explain everything that you need to know without blinding you with science. Sailing terminology has been reined-in as much as possible and only information relating to jib trimming has been included. We have not tried to explain tactics, navigation, strategy, main sail trimming, helming, spinnaker work, or any of the many other subjects you simply don't need to understand in order to be able to trim the jib well.

"Jib trimming is often referred to as a black art."

As you recoil in horror at the prospect of trying to achieve the unachievable, rest assured that with the information contained within this book, you will soon be trimming with confidence and ability. The guide is full of annotated photographs and diagrams that show you exactly what you're trying to achieve. We have also explained the many 'secrets' that help others stand out from the crowd. Once this guide is in your head, you will be trimming like a pro.

You're part of a team!

The jib trimmer is part of a team. Whether you're sailing on a two man dinghy or part of a team of thirty on an ocean racing yacht, there are many other responsibilities on the boat. While you are preoccupied with the jib, the helmsman is concentrating on steering the boat, the main sail trimmer is focused on the main sail, and the tactician is deciding where to go and warning the team of changing conditions. Others on the boat will be hoisting and dropping sails, handling spinnaker poles, moving their weight around and doing whatever they can to help. A key to doing well as a jib trimmer is to understand how you relate to the other core members of the team. This book highlights when and how you can expect others to act.

Section 1

Creating Lift and Avoiding Drag

Creating Lift with Airfoils

Before you start looking at sail shape, you must first understand a little of how sails work.

- Whilst a boat is sailing, its sails are its engines. Sails use wind energy to create driving force. This force is harnessed to move a boat through (and sometimes over) the water.

- Sails can be used as airfoils or air dams. The jib is mostly used for upwind sailing and this is when it's used as an airfoil. Down wind sailing means the sail is used as an air dam. The cross-over point is, approximately, when you're sailing on a broad reach (see Appendix C).

- Airfoils are special shapes that create lift and drag. Lift is the useful force that we use to make the boat go forward. Drag represents the forces that slow the boat down. Good sail trimming is about maximizing lift and minimizing drag.

Having promised not to blind you with science, there is a little bit of theory you can't do without if you're going to understand lift and drag. It's pretty straight forward though!

- Higher pressure air tries to move towards lower pressure air. Anything between high and low pressure experiences a force towards the lower pressure too. For example, when you burst a balloon, the higher pressure air inside the balloon escapes. As it does so, the outside of the balloon is blown away – towards lower pressure air.

- The same principle applies to airfoils such as airplane wings or sails.

- Airfoils are used to create a pressure difference. This pressure difference generates lift. Lift is a force that we harness in sailing to make a boat move forwards. In aviation, this force is harnessed to elevate aircraft.

Airfoil: Airplane Wing

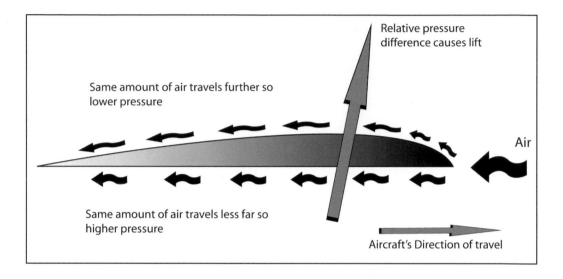

The engines on an airplane move the plane forward. This causes air to flow over the wings. There is a relative difference between the speeds at which the same amount of air travels over the wing compared to under. This is because the air traveling over the wing has further to travel. This relative difference in speed causes a pressure difference that lifts the wing, and with it the airplane.

Airfoil: Sail

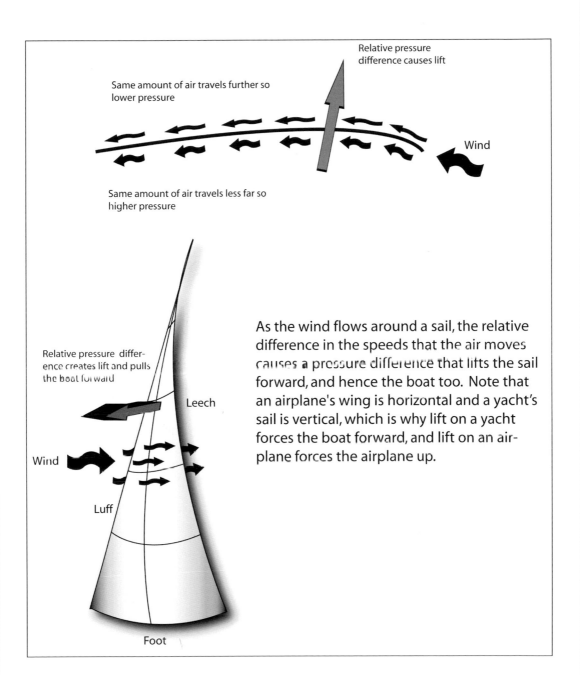

Relative pressure difference causes lift

Same amount of air travels further so lower pressure

Wind

Same amount of air travels less far so higher pressure

Relative pressure difference creates lift and pulls the boat forward

Leech

Wind

Luff

Foot

As the wind flows around a sail, the relative difference in the speeds that the air moves causes a pressure difference that lifts the sail forward, and hence the boat too. Note that an airplane's wing is horizontal and a yacht's sail is vertical, which is why lift on a yacht forces the boat forward, and lift on an airplane forces the airplane up.

Avoiding Drag with Airfoils

Now that you understand lift, let's look at drag.

- Drag sounds bad - and it is bad. Too much drag will cause the boat to become less controllable and it will go slower as a result.

- Drag is created as a side-effect of lift and it primarily causes a boat to be knocked over. This is called heeling. While a bit of heel is often good, too much slows the boat down. The more a boat heels, the more the helmsman will have to compensate with the rudder. The more the helmsman uses the rudder, the slower the boat goes since it ends up acting like a brake.

- On a windy day out on the water, many boats will have much too much heel, i.e. over 20 degrees. Many will have over 60 degrees of heel and some will almost be flattened. This is bad sailing and is entirely avoidable. As a jib trimmer, you are part of a team that controls the balance between lift and drag.

- When a boat is sailing well, it is because we have created the right balance in the sails between lift and drag. Section 3 explains the fundamentals of jib sail shape. It is essential for you to understand what jib sail shapes there are and how you control them. With practice, you will immediately be able to see whether the sail is the right shape for the conditions.

To prepare you for Section 3, Section 2 will illustrate the jib, its place on the boat, the names of its controls, as well as giving you some important advice about using winches and cleats.

Section 2

The Jib and its Controls

Annotated picture of jib

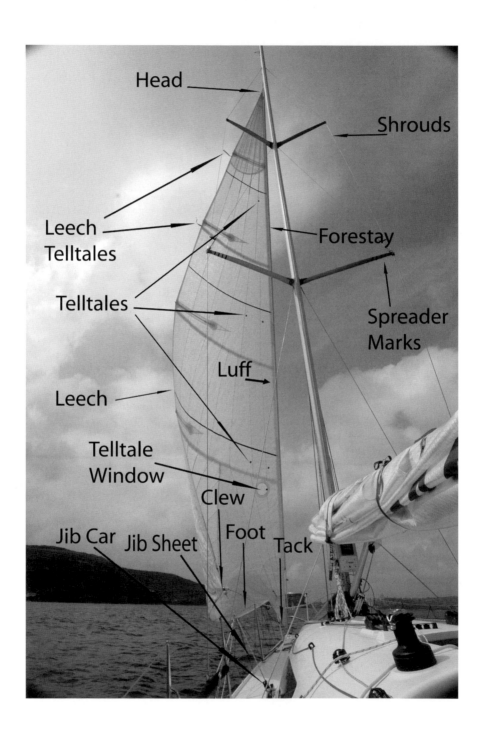

Jibs and Genoas

There is often confusion when people talk about jibs and genoas.

- There are several sizes of jib. The largest is often referred to as a genoa. This sail is called overlapping since it overlaps the mast. Typically, jibs come in sizes ranging from #1 to #4. The #1 is the biggest, i.e. a genoa, and the #4 is the smallest. The biggest sail, the genoa, is for the light winds and the smallest sail, the #4, is used for heavy winds.

- There's one more type of jib called a storm jib. This is much smaller than a #4 and is only used in over 30 knots of wind, including storm conditions.

- Larger racing yachts will tend to have a full range of jibs. Smaller boats sail with only one or two types of jib, and these are often not overlapping, and so are not referred to as genoas.

- To help you identify which sail you should be using, sails are generally labelled for their wind range, i.e. Light, Light/Medium, Medium, Medium/Heavy, and Heavy. Different sail makers have different ranges for each of their sails. If the sails aren't already labeled, or if the boat doesn't have a chart indicating wind ranges for each of the jibs, you must ask the sail maker.

We can't guess what type of boat you're going to be sailing on so we will generalize. The ideas that we're going to cover are applicable to all jibs. To be clear, we will stick to referring to fully over-lapping jibs as genoas and non-overlapping jibs as jibs.

Winches

Winches make trimming easier by allowing you to pull much harder on a rope than you could without it. Although you probably don't need a winch in very light winds, you will as soon as the wind picks up.

- Winches are used for jib trimming in almost all yachts. Dinghies and other small sail boats don't usually have winches since the loads developed in the ropes aren't all that high.

- Winches are always operated in the same way. A rope is wrapped clockwise around the winch two or more times. A winch handle is used to turn the winch while you keep tension on the end of the rope. Winches are often two-speed. This means that if you turn the winch handle one way it's easier but the rope won't be pulled in as fast. Turning the handle in the opposite direction is harder but you can get the rope in faster.

- As a rule of thumb, and if you need to get the rope in fast, always turn the handle the fast way until it becomes too hard. Then turn the handle the other way to finish the job.

- For the jib trimmer, the boat's primary winches are used for the jib sheets. The jib halyard should also be on a winch on the cabin top where small adjustments can be made to halyard tension.

- One of the most important tricks to know is how to get the winch handle out in a hurry. Practice this until you're confident you can do it every time. The secret is to grasp the handle where it enters the winch, flick the lever with your thumb and then pull the handle straight up out of the winch. A good tip is to keep the leaver greased.

- It's very important to only turn the winch handle in full circles. Do not develop the bad habit of ratcheting the winch one way then the other. This will damage the winch.

- If the winch does not turn smoothly, suggest to the skipper that some maintenance is required.

- If you aren't using the winch handle (or aren't about to) you should stow it in its proper place out of harm's way.

Cleats

Cleats are used to stop ropes slipping once they've been trimmed on. There are many different types of cleat but they all do the same thing.

- Cleats used for the jib sheet are likely to be either clam cleats, or the cleats on the top of self-tailing winches.

- Being able to trim or ease a sheet quickly and with little warning is often necessary. Self-tailing winch cleats are very cumbersome and can add many seconds on to easing or trimming sheets, especially if the winch handle is in the winch. Therefore, if there's a choice about whether to use a clam cleat or a self-tailing winch cleat, use the clam cleat. This will enable you to leave the winch handle in whilst sheeting out. Similarly you can trim the sheet by winching and holding onto the rope to keep the rope coils snug around the winch. Taking this approach means there is almost no time between decision and action.

- On longer passages when racing or cruising, and if you're not going to alter jib trim very often, it's o.k. to use the self-tailing cleat in the top of the winch.

- Ropes are cleated into clam cleats by pulling the rope towards you and down through the jaws of the cleat.

- Ropes are un-cleated from clam cleats by pulling the rope towards you and up out of the cleat.

- There's a third type of cleat called a jam cleat. These can be found on older boats and are operated by simply pulling the rope into the cleat's jaws. These are often worn and ineffective, causing ropes to come loose at the least desirable times. If at all possible, have these replaced with clam cleats.

Clam Cleat vs. Self-tailing Winch

Clam Cleat

The jib sheet is wrapped around the winch then cleated using a clam cleat. This technique enables you to quickly release the jib sheet to ease or trim the sheet. This is the most desirable approach for responsive jib trimming.

Self-tailing Winch Cleat

In this photograph, the jib sheet is wrapped around the winch and then cleated in the top of the winch using the self-tailing mechanism. This takes longer to un-cleat and so adds time to a quick ease or trim. Consequently, and unless you're sailing on a long leg of a race or cruising, this technique is not advisable to use.

On larger boats, you should have two or more turns more than shown in this photograph. This is because the high loads in the sheet can easily bend the chrome feeder in anything but light winds.

Hoisting the Jib

The jib is hoisted by pulling on the halyard. When hoisting the jib, make sure that the person doing the hoisting (at the mast or in the cockpit) is looking forward at the sail. It's easy to have part of the jib caught on the way up. For example, on a wire forestay hanks can get jammed around the swage at the bottom of the forestay. Other parts of the jib may get caught on a hatch or a cleat. If the person blithely hoisting doesn't see this happening, the sail will be damaged.

Once the jib has been hoisted, it's important that it has the right amount of tension. As you will discover in the next chapter, halyard tension controls the position of the belly of the sail, which in turn affects 'groove'.

An easy way to achieve repeatable settings is to mark the jib luff and the forestay. Each time the jib is hoisted, the marks on the sail are compared to the mark on the forestay by the person hoisting at the mast.

- If a tight halyard is required, the bottom mark on the jib will align with the mark on the forestay (or luff groove).

- If a very loose halyard is required, the top mark on the jib will align with the mark on the forestay (or luff groove).

- If medium tension is required, the middle mark of the jib will align with the mark on the forestay (or luff groove).

- Instructions for setting up the marks on the jib and forestay (or luff groove) are contained in Appendix A.

As you will see, these marks won't just be useful when hoisting - as conditions change, you will need to alter many of the controls, including the jib halyard.

Section 3

Sail Shape

Overall Jib Trimming Goals and Means

Now that you've covered the basics of lift and drag, the sail and its associated controls, it's time to understand sail trim.

Goals:
- To develop as much lift as possible to go as fast as possible.
- To reduce drag until the boat is manageable and going fast.

Therefore, the correct sail shape is the best compromise between lift and drag.

Means:
The power in the sails is controlled in two ways: rig setup (shroud tension, backstay tension) and jib trim (sheets, halyards, jib car).

1) Rig Setup

- Rig tension is controlled by the skipper, though the job of making changes to the rig may have been delegated - perhaps even to you! The purpose of changing the rig tension is to control the overall power that the sails can develop.

- You're in big trouble if your rig's out by very much. Racing in light winds with a rig set up for big winds will see you wallowing at the back of the fleet. A rig set up for light winds but sailed in heavy winds might see you sailing wildly out of control.

- When you're racing, the rules tend to limit the changes you're allowed to make to the rig. Changes to the rig can only be made before the preparatory period of a race.

- Importantly though, the backstay can be changed throughout a race.

What does this mean to you as the jib trimmer?

- However well you trim your jib, you cannot develop more lift from the sails than is available from the rig. Since your job is to help make the boat sail well, you need to be aware that poor performance may be coming from somewhere else on the boat. If the boat is going slower than expected, and perhaps the blame is being leveled at you or the main sail trimmer, the following question needs to be asked: is the backstay on too much? Is the rig too tight for these conditions??

2) Jib trim

- The second means of controlling power in the sails is the subject of the rest of the book.

Read on to understand the concepts of jib trim…

Sail Shape: Belly (Depth)

Sail depth, or belly size, controls the power in the sail, and hence how much lift and drag is created.

- The sail is at its most powerful, and creating most lift, when its belly is at its biggest setting. However, sailing with a big belly in high winds creates too much drag, which causes the boat to heel over, become uncontrollable and slow down.

- A big belly is suitable for light winds and a small belly is suitable for strong winds. You reduce the size of the belly as the winds get stronger but you only start reducing the belly as the forces of drag affect your performance and start to slow you down. As the wind drops in strength, you increase the belly again.

There are three sets of controls that affect the overall size of the belly: the rig, the jib car and the halyard.

- Rig tension limits overall power and cannot be adjusted whilst racing. The backstay also limits overall power (within the boundaries set by the rig tension) but can be adjusted whilst racing. The harder the backstay is tensioned, the tighter the forestay becomes and so the flatter the sail becomes. The looser the back stay, the looser the forestay and so the more powerful the jib.

As jib trimmer, you only have direct control over the jib car and halyard.

- Moving the car forward provides more belly and therefore more power.

- Moving the car back provides less belly and therefore less power.

- Tightening the halyard flattens the sail and so reduces power. Loosening the halyard increases the depth of the sail and creates more power. The halyard also affects groove as you will see later on.

As a member of a team of sailors, you should ask the skipper before you start sailing what the rig tension is being set to. After all, it affects you as well as the rest of the boat.

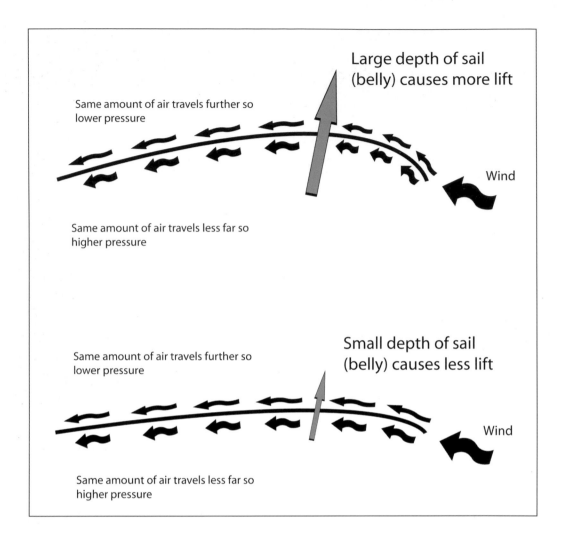

Large depth of sail (belly) causes more lift

Same amount of air travels further so lower pressure

Wind

Same amount of air travels less far so higher pressure

Small depth of sail (belly) causes less lift

Same amount of air travels further so lower pressure

Wind

Same amount of air travels less far so higher pressure

A deeper sail (bigger belly) produces more lift and drag. A sail with a smaller belly creates less lift and drag. Although the lift is welcome, in higher winds the drag overpowers the boat and makes it uncontrollable and slow. Therefore, we vary the depth of the sail according to the wind strength.

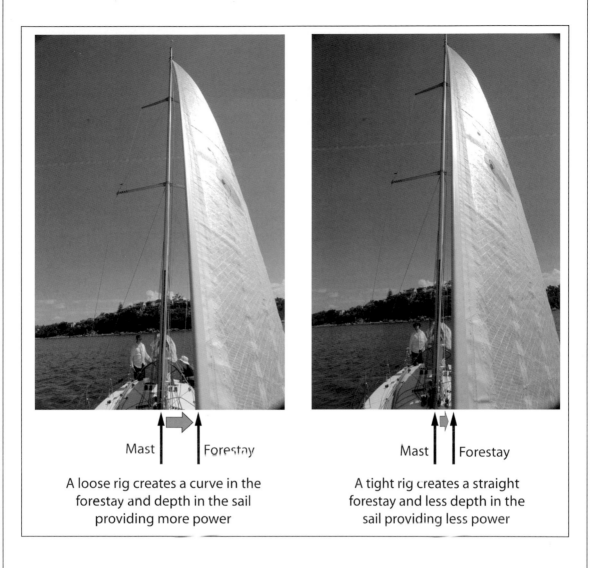

A loose rig creates a curve in the forestay and depth in the sail providing more power

A tight rig creates a straight forestay and less depth in the sail providing less power

Although the difference between a loose and tight rig is hard to see, the effect is significant in terms of the overall power the sail generates. A quick and easy way to check the rig tension's affect on forestay tension, and therefore overall power in the jib, is to grab the forestay and push against it. A tight forestay will hardly yield whereas a loose forestay will move appreciably.

When you are sailing, you should make it your business to know how tight the rig is. As you will see, rig tension not only affects the overall power in the sail but also affects where the belly is, but more on that later.

Sail Shape: Groove

Groove is a measure of how easy the boat is to sail in waves. A wider groove and more depth enables the helmsman to steer through a greater range of angles, which is necessary when sailing through waves. Although we need groove to help us steer, we do not want to use so much of it that we loose power.

- Groove is affected by how close the belly of the sail is to the luff and its position is controlled by the jib halyard. Tightening the jib halyard moves the belly towards the luff, thus widening the groove. Easing the halyard moves the belly back and in so doing narrows the groove.

- An unwanted side-affect of increasing groove by tightening the halyard is that the sail will become flatter and will therefore have less power to get through the waves. You need to achieve the best compromise between the helmsman being able to steer and the boat having enough power.

- It's easy to judge how much groove a sail has simply by looking at it. If the front of the luff is rounded, the sail has a wide groove. If the front of the luff is flat, the sail has a narrow groove.

- A quick way of repeatably getting near the right setting is to mark the jib luff and forestay (or luff groove) as detailed in the previous section. (See Appendix A for an explanation on how to set up the marks.)

- The way to determine whether you have sufficient groove is by talking to the helmsman. If you're sailing through waves, check that the boat is sailing well. If the boat's not sailing well, the chances are that you need to increase the width of the groove. Rather than tightening the halyard so the belly goes right to the front of the luff, start by moving the belly half way from the middle of the sail to the luff. After 20 seconds, ask how the boat is sailing. If it's sailing well, make a note of the luff's position against the forestay mark. If it's not quite right, repeat this process until the boat is sailing well.

- On some boats, a jib cunningham is also available. This is much easier to adjust when you're under sail. For groove purposes, both the jib cunningham and the jib halyard have the same effect. If there isn't a jib cunningham, ask whether it might be possible to have one fitted. Some class rules will prohibit it but others will not.

- As jib trimmer, you must change the jib halyard (or jib cunningham) to suit the conditions. It may actually be someone else that makes the change but it's your sail, so you're in charge!

- As a member of the team, you must talk to the helmsman to find out whether you should increase or decrease the groove in the sail. If you notice the helmsman struggling to steer a straight course in waves, ask whether some assistance is required. If you've previously tightened the halyard and the water becomes flat, ask whether you can ease the halyard. You can be sure that everyone else will forget that the halyard has been tightened when the waves have died down.

Groove and Rig Tension

It's important to understand that groove is also affected by rig tension.

- A slack rig results in a loose forestay, which in turn results in the belly moving forward. This results in a wider groove. To compensate, you will need to move the belly back again by further loosening the halyard.

- A tight rig results in a tight forestay, which in turn results in the belly moving back. This produces a narrower groove and so you will need to further tighten the halyard in order to bring the belly forward again.

You might remember that rig tension is partially set before a race (shroud tension etc.) but it's also changed constantly throughout a race with the back stay. This means that you must constantly evaluate whether the belly is set in the right place.

A word of warning though: sails made of modern composite materials may permanently deform if the halyard is too tight, e.g. stretched by more than 1% of the luff length – this would not please the person paying for the sails!

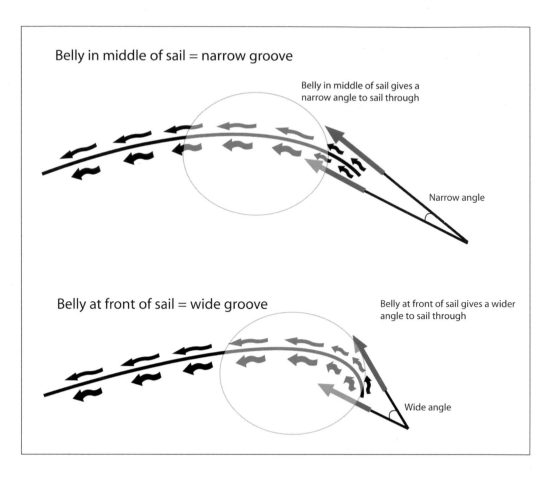

Tightening the halyard moves the sail's belly forward and so increases the angles you may sail through. This is called 'groove'.

- You need a wide groove for waves where you can't sail in a straight line.

- On flat water, you should sail with a narrower groove since you can sail in a straight line.

You need to sail with as narrow a groove as the helmsman can steer. This is because a looser halyard provides more belly and therefore more power.

Sail Shape: Groove

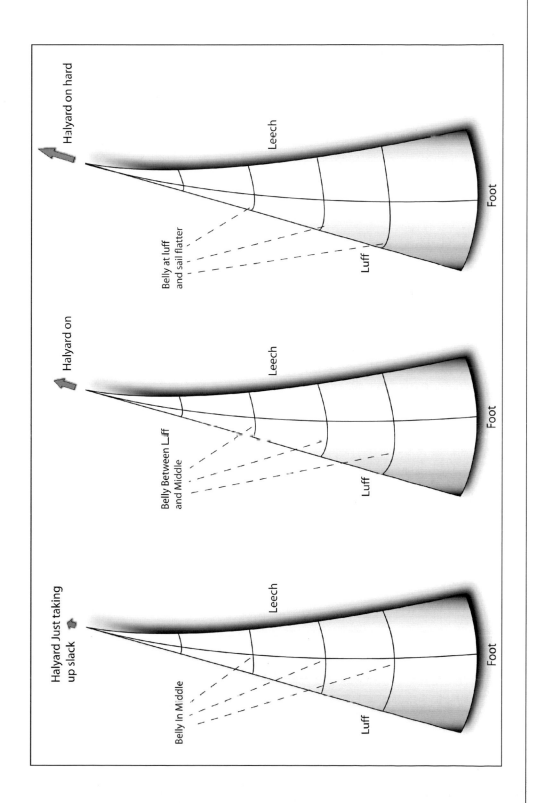

Halyard Just taking up slack

Belly In Middle

Leech

Luff

Foot

Halyard on

Belly Between Luff and Middle

Leech

Luff

Foot

Halyard on hard

Belly at luff and sail flatter

Leech

Luff

Foot

Photographs of Belly Position (Groove)

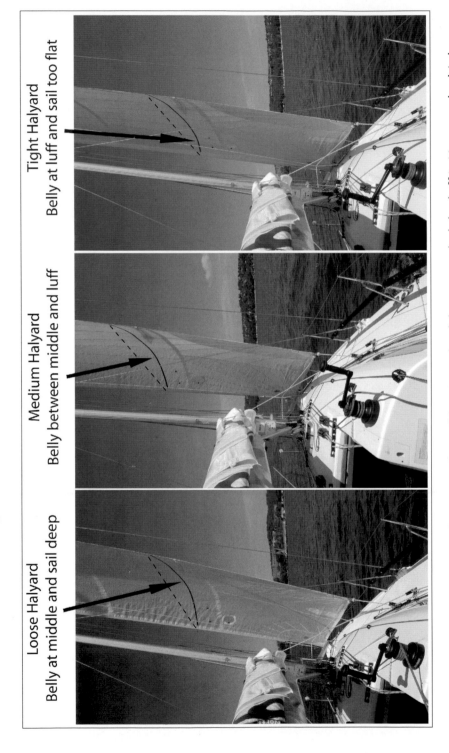

Loose Halyard
Belly at middle and sail deep

Medium Halyard
Belly between middle and luff

Tight Halyard
Belly at luff and sail too flat

The trick to seeing how much groove the sail has is to check how rounded the luff is. You can do this by running your eyes along the horizontal line on the jib. We've added a dotted straight line so you can see the effect that the halyard has on depth: too much halyard reduces depth and therefore power.

Sail Shape: Foot

The jib car affects the belly at the jib's foot. You might remember that the belly in the rest of the sail is controlled overall by rig tension, including the backstay.

- The shape of the foot determines how much power the lower third of the sail generates. In light winds the belly should be big, in medium winds the shape should be smaller, and in high winds it should be flat. In very light (drifting) winds when the wind struggles to get around the sails, the belly should also be flat.

- Understanding how much belly there is at the jib foot is easy. After you have sheeted the sail in, the biggest belly will see the foot touching (or almost touching) the lifelines on the side of the boat. The smallest belly will be flat, i.e. a straight line from the tack to the clew. Medium belly sizes are in between these two extremes.

- You might notice that the jib car can go further back from the setting that provides a flat foot. This is to allow the car to go so far back that the leech opens completely. This is for heavy winds and is discussed in the next section.

- The position of the jib car also affects how hard the jib sheet pulls down on the leech. The further forward the car goes the more directly the jib sheet pulls down on the leech and causes the leech to close. The further back the jib car goes the less down-force the jib sheet exerts. This particular point should just sit in the back of your mind for the time being: the main point to understand is that the car affects the belly at the sail's foot. Getting confused about this is what makes people believe that jib trimming is a black art.

Sail Shape: Foot

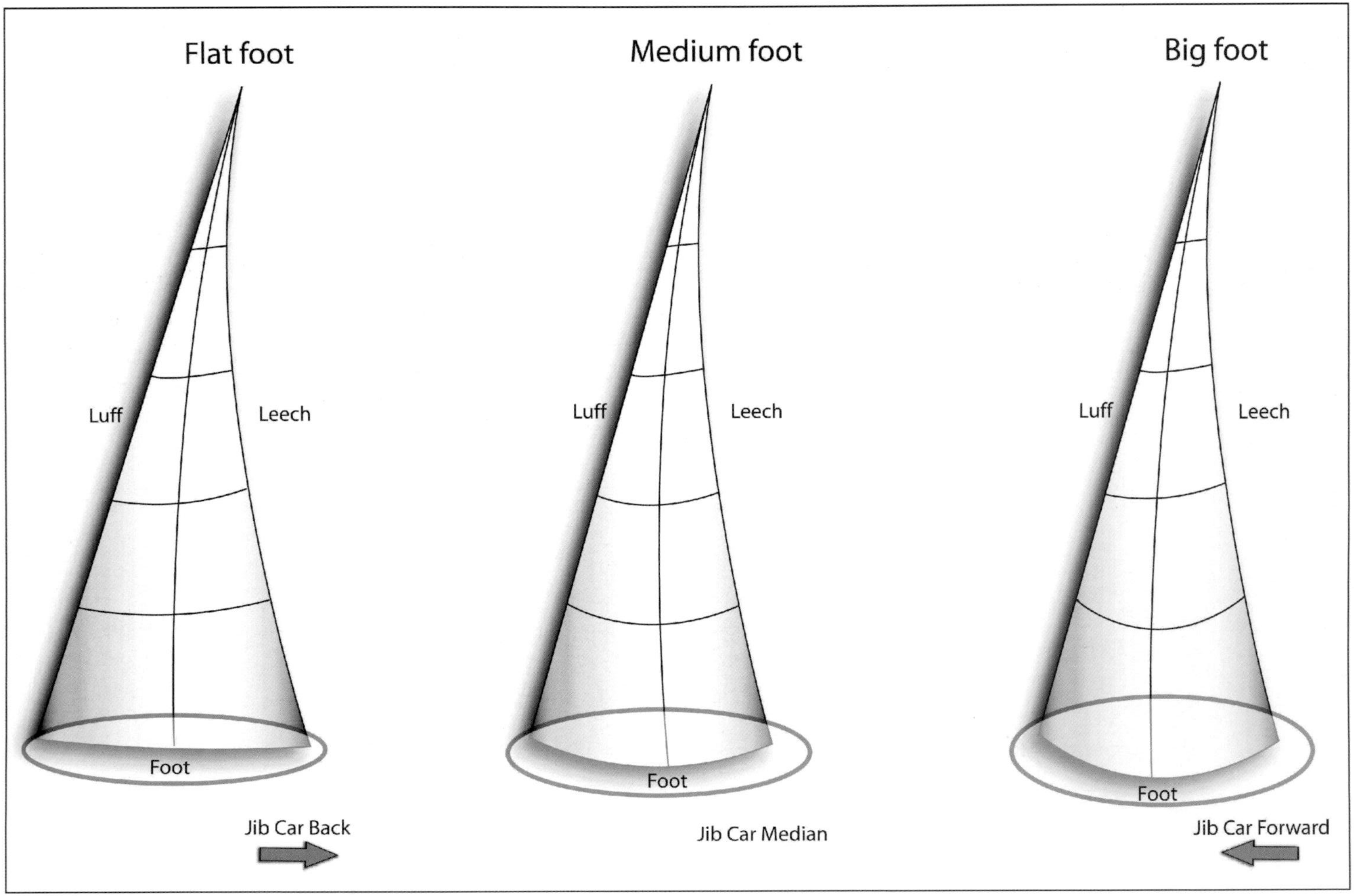

Flat foot

Leech

Luff

Foot

Jib Car Back

Medium foot

Leech

Luff

Foot

Jib Car Median

Big foot

Leech

Luff

Foot

Jib Car Forward

Photographs of Foot Size

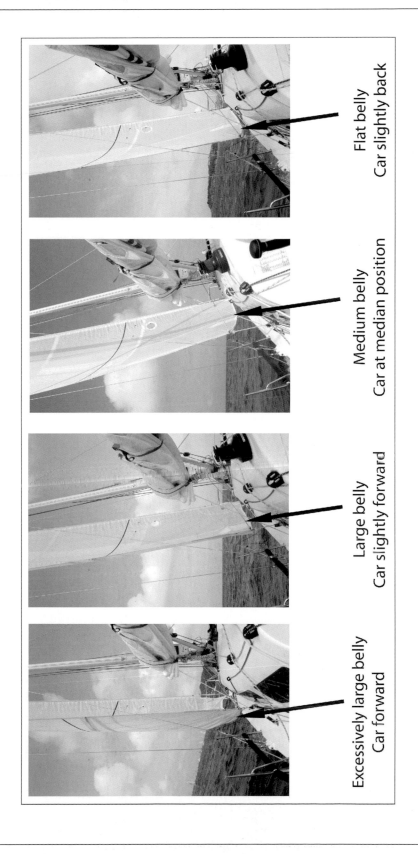

Flat belly
Car slightly back

Medium belly
Car at median position

Large belly
Car slightly forward

Excessively large belly
Car forward

Sail Shape: Leech (Twist)

The shape of the jib's leech is referred to as twist. If the leech at the top of the sail is angled further out from the boat than at the foot, we say it is open and therefore has twist. The amount of twist simply refers to how open, or closed, the top of the leech is.

- Understanding how much twist is in the sail is easy. By looking up at the leech from the low side of the boat, you can simply see where the leech is by gauging its position with the first (or maybe only) spreaders.

- For a jib, the key to quickly finding the right amount of twist is to mark the spreaders with black bands using electrical tape. The inboard mark indicates the least twist; the outboard mark indicates the most twist. The one or two middle marks indicate medium degrees of twist.

- For a genoa, the key is to judge how far the leech is from the spreader tip. The least possible twist is when the sail is touching the spreader tip. The most twist is when the sail is approximately 12 inches off the spreader tip, though this figure varies depending on the sail and the size of boat. It's likely that a larger boat will have a maximum twist of more than 12 inches off the spreader tip.

- Twist is affected by the jib sheet. The tighter the jib sheet, the less twist, and hence the more closed the top of the leech becomes.

- Different wind and sea conditions call for different amounts of twist. Light and very light winds require lots of twist. Medium and strong winds call for little or no twist. Heavy winds require one of two things: either the leech needs to be so twisted that the wind simply spills out of the top of the sail. Or, you must change down to a smaller jib and/or reef the mainsail.

- Sailing in waves requires more twist, more power and more groove than sailing on flat water. This helps keep the boat sailing as it is rocked around by the waves. In other words, at the same time as you widen the groove by tightening the jib halyard (or jib cunningham), you will also need to ease the jib sheet slightly. You should also move the jib car slightly forward too – more so than for the same wind on flat water.

Sail Shape: Leech (Twist)

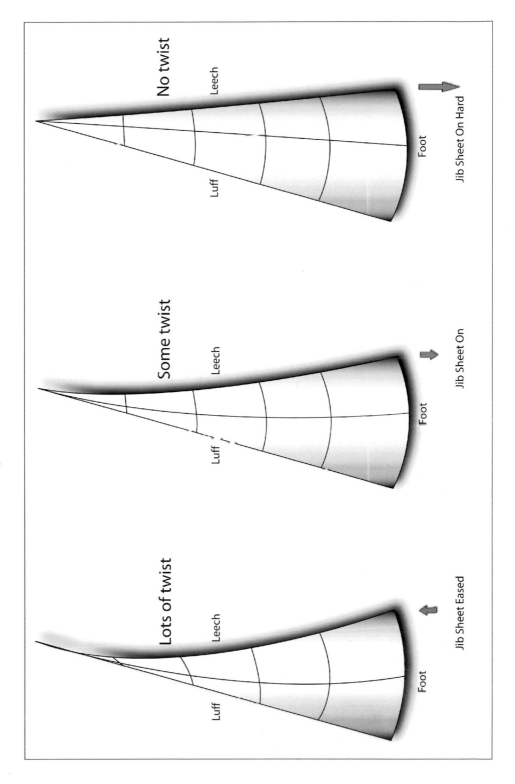

No twist
Leech
Luff
Foot
Jib Sheet On Hard

Some twist
Leech
Luff
Foot
Jib Sheet On

Lots of twist
Leech
Luff
Foot
Jib Sheet Eased

Photographs of Leech (Twist)

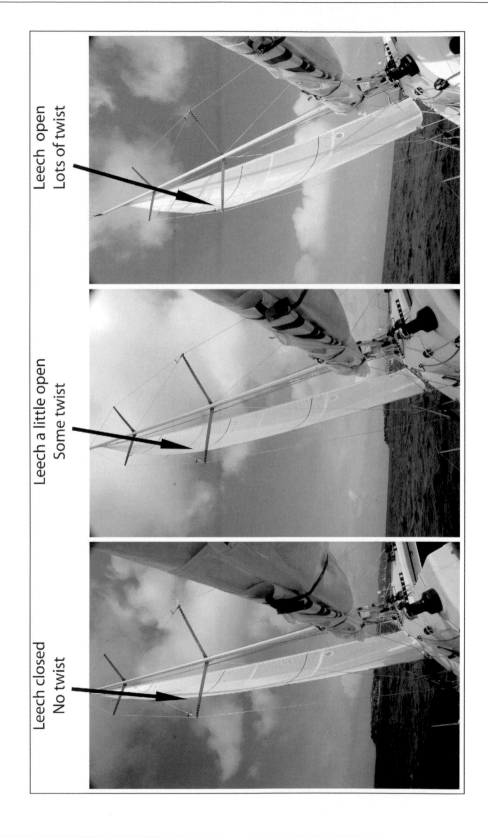

Leech open
Lots of twist

Leech a little open
Some twist

Leech closed
No twist

The Complete Shapes

Now that you have covered the concepts of belly size and twist, it's time to put them together:

- In very light airs, the wind will be struggling to get around the sail. Therefore, you create a flattish foot to prevent the wind from stalling. So, the car should be at or slightly back from the median position. The leech must be twisted so the sheet should be moderately eased.

- In light airs, the wind will be able to get around the sail, so maximum belly is wanted, therefore the car should be forward of the median position. The leech must be twisted so the sheet should be eased.

- In medium airs, you no longer want full power from the sail. Therefore the foot should have a medium to small belly, so the car should be at the median position (or further back for stronger airs). The leech should be fairly closed so the sheet should be trimmed on hard.

- In strong winds, a flat foot is needed, so the car should be even further back from the median position. The leech setting will depend on just how strong the wind is. If the boat is over-powered with the leech closed (sheet trimmed on hard), then it's time to radically twist off the top of the leech by moving the jib car well back and easing the sheet a little. With the genoa, there's another option in strong winds. To de-power and keep the boat on its feet, you can ease the sheet until the genoa touches the lifelines. This must be done at the same time as easing the main.

In overall terms, jib trimming is simple. The challenge is to remember these shapes and fine tune with the telltales. We recommend that you download, print, laminate and stick the next page in the cockpit for quick reference. See Appendix B for download details.

The Complete Jib Shapes

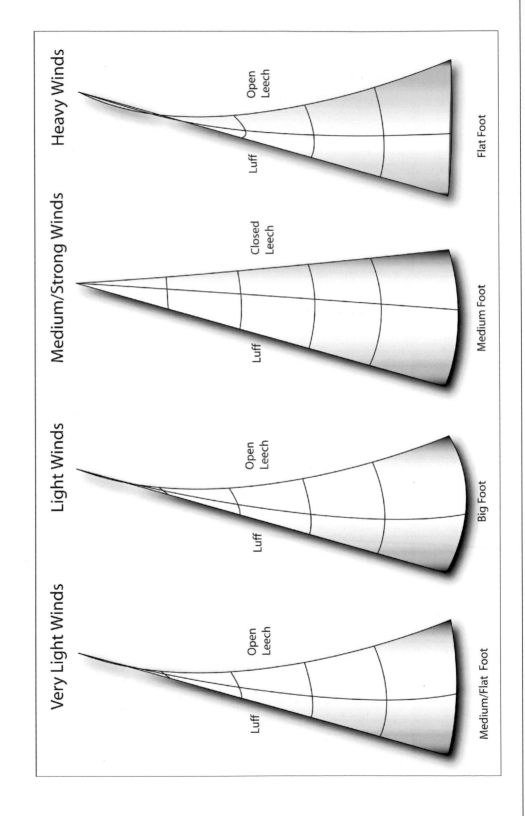

Photographs of Complete Shapes

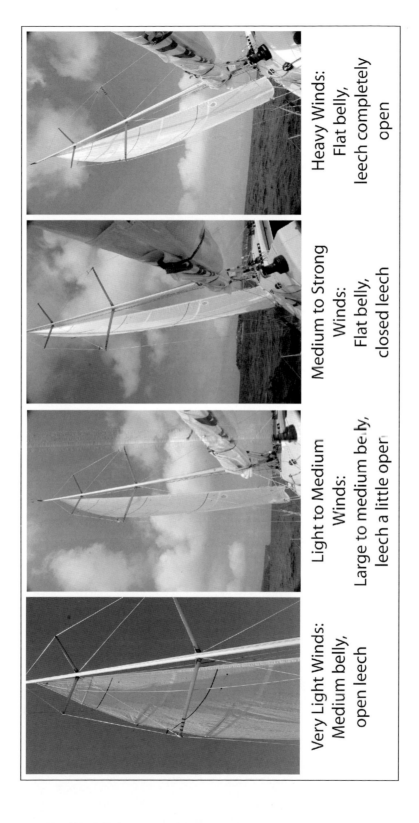

Heavy Winds:
Flat belly,
leech completely open

Medium to Strong Winds:
Flat belly,
closed leech

Light to Medium Winds:
Large to medium belly,
leech a little open

Very Light Winds:
Medium belly,
open leech

Reading the Telltales

The telltales tell us exactly what the wind is doing on the jib, and hence whether our twist is correct. If the twist is wrong, not all of the telltales along the luff of the jib will be flying.

- You should use the black bands on the spreaders to see the approximate setting for twist in the jib. For the genoa, the distance between the spread tip and sail should be used. However, the true measure of twist is in the telltales.

- Our aim is to have the whole of the jib sailing, not just the middle. With the jib car in the right position, you fine tune the twist with the sheet. If the inside top telltale is stalling whilst the middle telltales are flowing evenly on both sides of the sail, trim the sheet on. If the outside top telltale is lifting, ease the sheet. If they're flowing evenly up and down the luff on both sides, you've achieved your goal – for that particular moment at least!

- The exception to this rule is sailing in heavy airs. This is when you completely open this leech at the top of the sail to spill wind and avoid being over-powered. Then, and because the top of the sail isn't sailing anymore, the telltales can't tell us anything useful.

- If you can't trim the sail so all the telltales fly as expected, you have almost certainly got the car in the wrong position. Another possibility is that the sail is too stretched and it's time to buy a new one.

- On some jibs, telltales are fitted along the leech. These also tell us whether the wind is flowing evenly along both sides of the jib. If the telltale is wrapping around the outside of the sail then that part of the jib is over trimmed. If the telltale is wrapping around the inside of the sail then that part of the jib is under trimmed.

Photographs of Telltale Reading

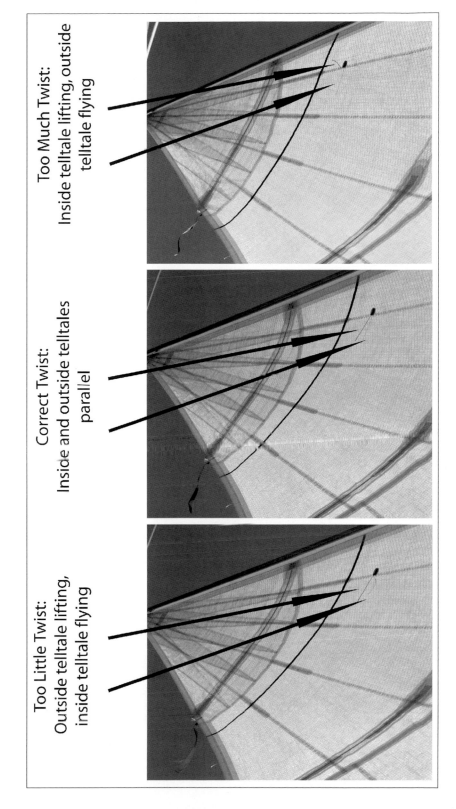

Too Little Twist:
Outside telltale lifting, inside telltale flying

Correct Twist:
Inside and outside telltales parallel

Too Much Twist:
Inside telltale lifting, outside telltale flying

Section 4

Everything Changes All of the Time

Everything Changes All of the Time

- Wind speed and direction are rarely constant

- The sea state is rarely constant

- The boat changes speed after every tack, wave, wind change, gust and lull

Good jib trimming is all about knowing what to do every time something changes. There aren't that many controls (sheet, jib car and halyard), but knowing what to do and when to do it makes all the difference.

Tacking

Tacking is when the boat is turned through the wind from one 'tack' to the other. Good tacking depends on coordination and trim.

- Before the tack, make sure the old sheet will be able to run as soon as it comes off the winch. Also, ensure the winch handle is out of the winch.

- Ensure the new sheet is loaded onto the winch on the other side of the boat and the winch handle is in place.

- When tacking, don't let the old sheet go until the sail starts to collapse.

- In light wind it pays to let the jib 'back' a little before releasing the sheet. This helps to get the bow of the boat through the wind without using too much rudder. Backing is when the jib tries to fill on the new side whilst still attached on the old side (see picture on next page).

- After the boat has gone through the wind, pull on the new sheet as fast as possible. The next step is crucial: don't sheet the sail on hard until the boat has built up speed again. You're either in first or second gear. You must wait until the boat has accelerated before sheeting all the way in – see the next section on gears.

- Tacking a genoa requires good coordination and help from the crew. One of the crew (probably foredeck) needs to help by grabbing the sheets at the clew and guiding the sail around the mast. It's important to physically prevent the sail or the sheets from snagging on anything which will interfere with the tack. Make sure the old sheet is ready to run before the tack begins and that it's completely off the winch as you tack. Pulling on the new sheet needs to happen as fast as possible once the clew has cleared the mast.

Backing the Jib

In very light winds, it pays to back the jib to help the bow through the tack and avoids using excessive rudder. The jib sheet is held on the old side until the boat has almost completed the tack. As the tack completes, the new sheet is brought on sharply to get the sail trimmed and generating lift on the new side of the boat.

Using Gears

It's extremely useful to think of sailing as you think of using gears in a car. If you try to accelerate from 10 mph in top gear, you will fail, or at least take a very long time to go faster. It's the same with sailing. Top speed trim is different from starting trim. You can only get to top speed by going through two previous gears: starting and accelerating. Therefore, there are three main gears, and there's an overdrive too if you're sailing in flat water with a good breeze. Let's get there first though!

1st Gear: (when starting from scratch; at race start; after a large and unexpected wave; after a bad tack)

You ease the sheet a couple of inches and the helmsman steers down (away from the wind) until the middle telltales are flowing on the inside and outside of the sail. You stay in this gear until you've built up some speed, perhaps for 15 seconds.

2nd Gear: (after a good tack; after some waves that you've successfully footed through; at the start; during a lull; after 1st gear)

You trim the sheet on a bit more and the helmsman steers up (closer to the wind) until the middle telltales are flowing evenly on both sides of the sail.
You stay in this gear until you've built up some more speed, perhaps another 15 seconds.

3rd Gear: (after you've accelerated from 2nd gear; after a very good tack; at the start)

You trim the sails on fully and the helmsman steers up (towards the wind) until the outside telltales are flowing evenly and the inside telltales are flowing upwards at around 45 degrees.

Overdrive Gear: (after you've made it into 3rd gear)

On flat water and in good wind, the helmsman can steer even higher (closer to the wind), so the inside telltales are pointing almost vertically – this is our overdrive gear and is referred to as 'sailing lifted'.

Whether you can reach 2nd, 3rd and overdrive gear depends on the wind strength and sea state. If the wind is very light, you will stay in first gear. If the wind is just light, you might make it to 2nd gear. Only if there's enough wind, e.g. over 10 knots, will you be able to get into 3rd gear. Overdrive is only achievable in winds over approximately 14 knots and in flat water.

Using Gears

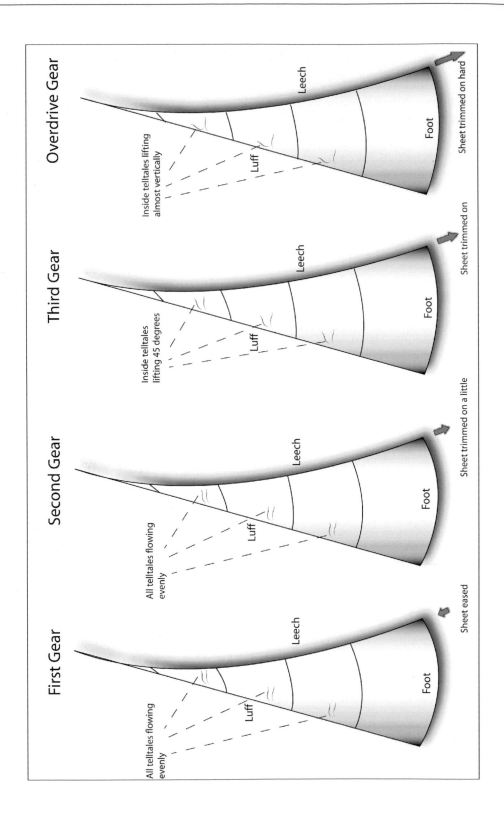

First Gear

All telltales flowing evenly

Luff

Leech

Foot

Sheet eased

Second Gear

All telltales flowing evenly

Luff

Leech

Foot

Sheet trimmed on a little

Third Gear

Inside telltales lifting 45 degrees

Luff

Leech

Foot

Sheet trimmed on

Overdrive Gear

Inside telltales lifting almost vertically

Luff

Leech

Foot

Sheet trimmed on hard

Photographs of Gears

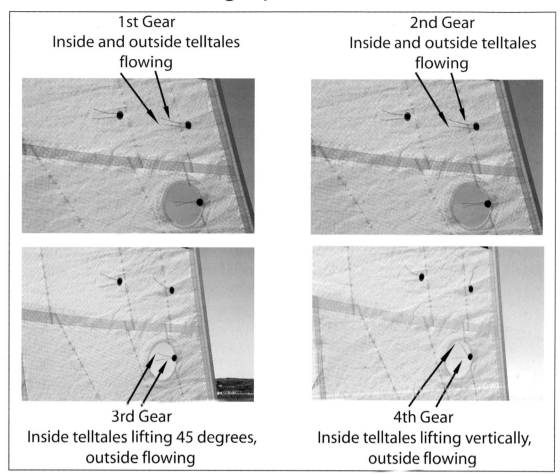

1st Gear
Inside and outside telltales
flowing

2nd Gear
Inside and outside telltales
flowing

3rd Gear
Inside telltales lifting 45 degrees,
outside flowing

4th Gear
Inside telltales lifting vertically,
outside flowing

The above photographs show the telltales at the middle of the sail.

It's hard to see the telltales on the outside of the sail. It's even harder depending on where the light's coming from. Even so, reading and understanding what the telltales mean is essential.

Footing

Footing means easing the sails a couple of inches and steering lower (further away from the wind) to gain power and speed. In terms of gears, you are deliberately stepping down a gear to power through choppy water.

Typical causes of localized choppy water are motor boat wakes.

- The cost of footing is having to point lower for a short time. The benefit is keeping speed - this is the best available compromise.

- You foot just before you hit some choppy water and as you're driving through it. If you don't foot and just keep on going, the boat will slow down dramatically and take a very long time to get back up to speed. Footing gives us the speed to drive through choppy water and minimize slowing down, and to accelerate again.

- Footing begins when you're given warning of impending chop. You ease the jib sheet a couple of inches and the helmsman steers down (away from the wind) just before the chop.

- You trim back on when you've accelerated after the chop and not before.

Motor boat wake

A motor boat's wake is an example of chop. Just before you hit the chop, you ease the jib sheet, sail a little lower (further from the wind) and power through.

Wind Changes

Wind changes occur for many reasons. The right course of action depends on what's happening to the wind at that particular time.

Shifts - when there's a gust or a lull

When the wind is under 8 – 10 knots, not everyone needs to be hiking-out. This usually means that you (the jib trimmer) can sit on the low side of the boat and trim all the time. This is a great opportunity for you to make significant improvements in boat speed by allowing you to respond appropriately to the changing conditions.

- During a gust, the increase in wind often manifests itself as a lift. This means that the boat is now pointing too low (too far away from the wind) and that the sail is now over-trimmed. The right course of action is for you to ease the sheet until the middle telltales flow evenly around both sides of the sail again. Then the helmsman points up (steers closer to the wind) and you trim the sails on again.

- The coordination for handling a lift from a gust requires concentration. Someone on the boat should be calling gusts, which gives everyone warning. When the gust hits, it might not become a lift. You need to look hard at the telltales to verify whether it is a lift, i.e. if the outside telltales are stalling whilst the inside telltales are flying. If you have been lifted, sheet out until the middle telltales are flowing on both sides of the sail. As the helmsman steers up towards the wind, you trim the sail back on again. Sheeting out when there is no lift is disastrous for boat speed!

- During a lull, the decrease in wind usually appears as a header (knock). The jib will start to collapse and the natural reaction for the helmsman is to bear away from the wind. This is usually the wrong course of action. Instead, the helmsman should continue to steer the same course. As the boat slows down to match the new lighter wind strength, the jib will start to fill again. Since you're now sailing in a lighter wind, you will need to ease the jib a little.

Stronger wind

- As the wind strength builds, you should trim the sail on harder to close the leech. This is unless you're overpowered and the foot is already flat. In which case, the jib car is moved even further back and the sheet is eased a little to fully open the top of the leech.

- When sailing in medium and stronger winds, car adjustments will probably have to wait for the next tack, since the jib car will be under considerable load. Therefore, make the change to the car position on the new side of the boat before you tack. Then, and if the wind holds its new strength, change the car on the other side after the tack.

- It is sometimes possible to move the car back under load. This will depend on your jib-track configuration. If you have control lines for the jib car, you should be able to move the car back under load, since the load in the sheet is trying to move the car back anyway.

- If you're sailing on one long tack and you can't move the car back under load, it's probably worth briefly easing the jib sheet to be able to move the car. This is because sailing with the car in the wrong position for a long period will do more harm to your performance than a brief ease of the sheet. Make sure you have someone help so you can minimize the time required to complete the operation.

- If the stronger wind means you're sailing outside the sail's wind range, consider a change down to a smaller jib.

Weaker wind

- Weaker wind also calls for a sail trim change. As we've discussed, and as the wind strength drops, you should ease the sheet to open the leech and deepen the lower half of the sail.

- The car should also be moved forward. Again, the position depends on the new wind strength. As above, and on long tacks, it's often worth changing the car position on the current tack. This will require a temporary ease of the sheet.

- If the weaker wind means you're sailing outside the sail's wind range, consider a change up to a bigger jib.

Sea State

Sea state affects your ability to sail the boat. The more waves there are, and the bigger they come, the harder it will be to sail the boat in a straight line.

- The way to overcome this problem is to tighten the halyard (or jib cunningham if you have one) to bring the belly of the sail forward. This increases the width of the groove, i.e. the angles the helmsman can sail through. Think of the halyard as 'groove control' or 'wave control'.

- The risk of increasing the width of the groove is that using too much halyard will flatten the sail and make it less powerful. As well as helping the helmsman steer through the waves, it's important to provide the boat with enough power to get through the waves.

- The key is to remember to change the setting as the sea state changes: more waves require more groove; fewer waves require less groove.

- As well as changing the groove settings, aggressive trimming and easing is required as the boat travels up and down waves. As the boat is steered up a wave (closer to the wind), the jib can be trimmed on slightly harder. As the boat is steered down the back of the wave (further away from the wind), the jib can be eased slightly.

Another unexpected feature of sailing in waves is the effect the wind has when it's coming from a slightly different direction to the waves.

- One tack will be harder to steer than the other because you will be traveling more directly into the waves.

- This means that the tack where you're sailing more directly into the waves will need more halyard (groove) and more twist (slightly eased sheet) than on the other tack. The other tack will be easier to steer and so you can ease the halyard and trim the sheet on harder than the other tack. Therefore, you must be aware which of these two tacks you're sailing on!

- The wavier tack will cause more bumping, and more water coming over the deck. Things will calm down on the other tack. Of course, knowing in advance will help. You should ask the skipper, the helmsman, or (if you have one) the tactician whether the sea is coming from the same direction as the wind.

Section 5

Offwind Trim

Offwind Trim: Reaching

All of the trim we've talked about so far has related specifically to close-hauled sailing (also referred to as beating or sailing as close to the wind as we can).

As soon as you bear away from close-hauled and start to sail off the wind, jib trimming becomes simpler but different, and a lot more physically demanding:

- The halyard will need to be eased a little if it was tight before.

- The jib cars will need to be moved forward. Not moving the car forward will cause the leech to fall open. This produces no lift and a lot of drag.

Gauging how far the jib car goes forward:

- Move the car forward and trim the sail so the middle telltales are flowing on both sides of the sail. Keep moving the car forward until the top of the leech begins to close. You will never be able to get the perfect shape: the top of the sail will be under-trimmed and the bottom over-trimmed. You should aim to get the top of the sail as under-trimmed as the bottom of the sail is over-trimmed. This compromise is necessary because the jib track is not ideally set-up for reaching,

- Some boats are fitted with jib tracks which are further out-board than the jib track you use for upwind sailing. If present, you should use these for reaching. Another option is to use snatch blocks. These are usually attached to the side of the boat and enable you to move the sheeting point further out-board. Taking either approach enables you to achieve a better, less compromised sail shape whilst reaching.

- Offwind trimming depends on whether the boat is being steered to the sails or on a course. You should ask the skipper which of the two approaches is being taken.

Sailing on a course, e.g. towards a mark:

Sailing on a course means that you will need to make constant adjustments to the sail

- If the middle telltales stall on the inside of the sail, sheet in

- If the middle telltales stall on the outside of the sail, case the sheet

Sailing to the telltales

In this case, the helmsman will be steering to keep the telltales flying on both sides of the sail. Only make an adjustment if asked to.

- If the helmsman tells you and the main sheet trimmer to head up (or trim on), wait until the main sheet trimmer has started to sheet in and then you trim the jib on until the middle telltales are both flowing. Having the main sheet trimmed on first helps to steer the boat closer to the wind without using as much rudder.

- If the helmsman asks you and the main sheet trimmer to head down (or ease the sheets), again wait for the main sheet trimmer to ease and for the boat to start bearing away (turning away from the wind). This has two benefits: keeping the jib trimmed on longer than the main helps turn the bow of the boat away from the wind, and easing the main allows the helmsman to bear away. Both benefits mean the helmsman can use less rudder.

Downwind Trim: Running

When sailing downwind (broad reaches or running), the telltales will no longer work. This is because the sails are no longer acting as airfoils and instead are working as air dams. Because the wind is no longer flowing evenly around the sails, the telltales will tend to hang limply.

Downwind sailing without a spinnaker requires one of two approaches. You either sail on broach reaches with the jib on the same side of the boat as the main sail or you can sail on broader reaches with the jib poled out on the opposite side of the boat. Of course, once we hoist the spinnaker, we usually drop the jib.

Sailing without a pole

- Sailing on broad reaches is the simplest and easiest way of sailing down wind. The jib is eased out until it starts to luff and then it's slightly trimmed on. If the jib moves further forward than the forestay, it's too far forward. To help stop the top of the leech from falling open, the jib car needs to be moved all the way forward. Most importantly, the jib stays on the same side of the boat to the mainsail. If a jibe is required to get to the downwind destination, the new jib sheet needs to be brought on during the jibe to prevent the sail from wrapping around the forestay. After the jibe is complete, the sheet is eased again until the jib luffs. As before, it needs to be trimmed on to prevent it from going past the forestay and to stop it from luffing. Make sure that the jib car is moved forward on both sides of the boat.

Goose winging

- Another tactic is to goose wing. This is where the jib is encouraged to sail on the opposite side of the boat to the main without a pole to hold it there. This is achieved by careful steering from the helmsman. For goose winging to work, the boat needs to be precariously close to jibing! To assist, you need to ensure that the jib is set correctly, i.e. not falling in front of the forestay and not trimmed too tight. If the sail starts to come back to the main sail's side of the boat, you might be able to catch it by sharply tugging the sheet.

| Spinnaker poll holds the jib out to expose more of the sail to the wind | No spinnaker poll means that less of the jib is exposed to the wind |

Sailing with a pole

Sailing with a pole is faster than sailing down wind without.

- The pole is hoisted and the jib sheet is attached to the end of the pole. The jib and pole are set on the opposite side of the boat to the main sail. This allows the jib to power up without being blanketed by the mainsail. To jibe you will need to ease the jib sheet so the pole can be detached. When the pole is set on the new side, trim the new sheet on until the jib's clew meets the end of the pole.

- It's important to get the right amount of downhaul on the pole. Again, our aim is to stop the leech from falling open. Have the downhaul pulled on until the leech closes.

- It's also important to have the pole out as far as possible, i.e. it needs to be set pointing straight out and perpendicular to the direction of the wind This ensures that you're using as much of the jib as possible.

- If the leech only closes when the downhaul pulls the pole so the pole is not level, i.e. the outboard end points down towards the water or up towards the sky, move the pole up or down at the mast to make it level.

Conclusion

Throughout this book we've talked about and illustrated the key concepts of jib trim. We've worked hard to get to the core principles that you need to understand to be able to trim the jib effectively. We've encouraged you to see shapes rather than learning figures. We've avoided jargon and shown that a black art is a simple and achievable art. Some things you need to do by yourself and other things involve some of the crew.

The art of jib trimming can be summarized as follows:

- **Understand what shape you need for the current conditions**

- **Understand how to achieve the right jib shape**

- **Don't ever stop trying to achieve the right shape since the conditions change all of the time**

- **Communicate with the helmsman, the main sheet trimmer and, if present, the tactician.**

That's it, good luck, but if you've followed closely, you won't need it!

Appendix A - Setting Up

If you're lucky, the car positions and leech settings will already be known and documented for your reference. If not, the easiest way to set up the track and leech is to get hold of a tuning guide from the sail maker. Tuning guides specify where everything related to the sails should go, including the jib cars and the leech.

Often this is not available, so the second best option is to get a representative from the sail maker to come on the boat and help you determine the right settings. This is standard service that you can expect if the sail maker thinks you might buy more of their sails.

If all of the above is not possible, the following pages explain how to do it yourself.

Spreader Marks

As mentioned earlier in this book, and if it hasn't been done already, you will need to mark the lower (or only) spreaders with electrical tape on both sides of the boat.

- First, measure the smallest distance between the mast and the jib track on the deck.

- Go up the mast and wrap electrical tape around the spreaders at the same distance from the mast that you just measured between the deck and jib track. Now wrap tape around the spreaders at roughly 3" intervals from the spreader tips towards the first inside mark.

- Make sure that the tape is well sealed and free from dust, grime or water to avoid having to go up the mast again any time soon.

Jib Track

Finding the jib car median position:

First, mark the jib track. Using an indelible marker, and starting from the front of the track, write numbers starting at 0 alongside the track. The numbers should go up in measures of the length of the car until you reach the end of the track. You will be able to use these numbers to quickly position the jib car correctly for each wind strength.

Next you need to find the car's median position.

- Sail the boat close hauled in around 8 knots of wind. Sheet out until the sail starts to collapse and then sheet back in until the sail has just stopped collapsing. The leech should be fairly open and is likely to be near the spreader tip.

- Have the helmsman luff the boat (steer closer to the wind so the sail starts to collapse).

- Check to see if the telltales break evenly up and down the luff as the jib begins to collapse

- If the top inside telltale stalls first, move the car forward. If the middle or bottom telltales stall first, move the car back.

- Keep testing by going through the steps above. The goal is to get the telltales breaking evenly with the top telltales just starting to lift first.

- Once known, all car settings are relative to this position. The car moves forward for lighter winds, and moves back for heavier winds. The car goes to median position for medium winds.

Make a note of this car position!

Marking the deck alongside the jib track enables you to quickly find the right car position for the conditions.

Genoa Track

Finding the genoa car median position:

The genoa track will either be a separate track further back on the boat or the back section of a very long track that services the jib and the genoa.

This is how to set up the genoa track yourself.

- First, mark the genoa track. Using an indelible marker, and starting from the front of the track, write numbers starting at 0 alongside the track. The numbers should go up in measures of the length of the car until you reach the end of the track. You will be able to use these numbers to quickly position the genoa car at the right position for each wind strength.

Next you need to find the car's median position. This is simpler to do than the jib track and is obtained as follows.

- As you're sailing close-hauled in light airs, position the car in the middle of the track. Sheet in until the sail touches the base of the shrouds or the spreader tip. The goal is to find the car position where the sail touches the shrouds and the spreader tip at the same time. If the sail touches the spreader tip first, move the car back. If the sail touches the shrouds first, move the car forward. Keep doing this until the sail touches the shrouds and the spreader tip at the same time.

Once you know what the median position is, all car settings are relative to this position. The car moves forward for lighter winds, and moves back for heavier winds. The car goes to median position for medium winds.

Jib Halyard

Setting up marks on the forestay (or luff groove) and the jib luff are essential for fast and repeatable settings when hoisting the jib or adjusting groove settings.

We recommend that you use a permanent marker on both sides of the jib.

The mark on the forestay will depend on how the jib's luff is attached. If the jib is attached directly to the forestay, you will need to stick some tape on the wire. If the jib is attached to the forestay using a luff groove, you should be able to use a permanent marker on the luff groove. Make sure you mark both sides. The goal is to make the marks visible to the person hoisting the sail at the mast.

Procedure for setting up the marks

Having first marked the forestay or luff groove at eye level when viewed standing at the mast, sail close-hauled in light to medium wind. Ease the halyard until horizontal wrinkles appear up and down the luff. Make sure you haven't eased the halyard to the point where the sail is not fully hoisted. Mark the jib on both sides to match the mark on the forestay (or luff groove).

Next, tighten the halyard until the wrinkles disappear. Mark the jib on both sides.

Finally, tighten the halyard until the belly just meets the luff and mark again. These are your three jib halyard settings.

See Section 2 (The Jib and its Controls) for an explanation on how to use these marks.

Appendix B - Trim Table Template

As we said earlier, without figures from the sail maker, it's impossible to be exact about wind ranges and sail trim on your boat. We have successfully generalized but the exact figures must come from you.

We recommend that you use the following table to help you be exact about the positions of the jib car. You can download a copy of the table from:

www.felixmarks.com

Print, complete and laminate the table, then stick it into the cockpit for quick reference.

Trim Table Template

Wind speed	0-5 knots Very Light	5-8 knots Light	8-16 knots Medium	16-25 knots Strong	25 knots + Heavy
Car	Median / Slightly Back	Median / Slightly Forward	Median / Slightly Back	Back	Fully Back
Genoa Leech	8" off	6" off	4" - 2" off	2" – 8" off	Use a jib
Jib Leech	Outside Band	Outside Band	Middle -> Inside Band	Inside -> Outside Band	Fully Open
Belly / Halyard	Forward in waves	Forward in waves	Forward in waves	Forward in waves	Forward in waves

Appendix C - Points of sail

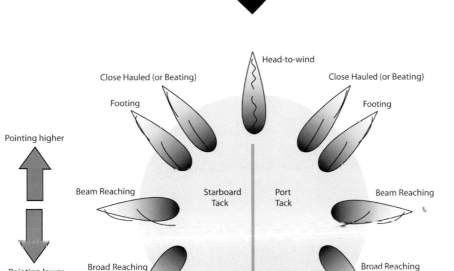

Glossary

Airs	A way of referring to wind strength, e.g. very light airs, light airs, medium airs, strong airs, heavy airs
Airfoil	A shape used to create lift, e.g. a sail or an airplane wing. Also known as an aerofoil
Belly	The fattest part of a sail also known as the draft
Beating	Sailing as close to the wind as possible, also known as sailing close-hauled
Back	Towards the back (stern) of the boat
Backing jib	When the jib is kept sheeted onto the old side of the boat during or after a tack. This is useful in light winds to avoid using too much rudder to turn the boat through the wind
Backstay	The wire running from the top of the mast to the back of the boat, which controls forestay tension (jib power) and main sail shape
Block	A pulley
Bow	The forward-most part of a boat's hull
Broad reaching	Sailing with the wind almost behind you (see Appendix C - Points of Sail)
Cleat	A device for making a rope fast, i.e. holding it and not letting it go despite the rope being under load
Clew	Corner of sail that a sheet is connected to
Close- hauled	Sailing as close as possible to the wind (also known as beating)
Closed	Typically referring to the top of the jib's leech and meaning little or no twist
Cunningham	An assembly that connects to the luff towards the bottom of the sail to apply down force to tighten the luff. For the jib its primary use is to bring the belly of the sail towards the luff and hence increase groove
Depth	The size of the sail's draft, also known as belly. More depth equals more power.

Down	A term used to indicate something further away from the wind (as opposed to up)
Downhaul	The line attached to the bottom of a pole used to pull the pole down
Drag	The side affect of lift that causes the boat to heel over and slow down
Ease	To sheet out or to loosen a rope, typically a sheet
Foot	The bottom edge of the sail
Forestay	The wire running from the mast to the front of the boat which has the jib's luff attached
Gust	A temporary increase in the wind
Halyard	A rope connected to the head (top) of a sail used to hoist the sail
Foot (1)	To turn slightly away from the wind whilst easing the sails, typically to power-up through chop
Foot (2)	The bottom edge of the sail
Footing	See Foot (1)
Forward	Towards the front (bow) of the boat
Genoa	A larger jib that overlaps (extends past) the mast
Header	When the wind changes direction disadvantageously and forces you to sail further away from your course than the old wind allowed. Also known as a knock
Headsail	A jib or genoa
Heel	The angle that a boat assumes as it is pushed over, whether by the wind or crew weight, or any other force
Helmsman	The person steering the boat, whether by tiller or by wheel
Jib	The front sail used on a yacht or a dinghy. Often referred to as a headsail
Jib car	The moveable assembly connected to the jib track that controls the size of the belly at the jib foot and the angle that the jib is sheeted at. The jib sheet runs through the block (pulley) which is attached to the jib car

Leech	The edge of the sail furthest back from the wind
Lift (1)	The useful force that an airfoil (such as a sail) creates
Lift (2)	When the wind changes direction advantageously and allows you to sail closer to your course than the old wind allowed
Luff (1)	The leading edge of a sail attached to the forestay
Luff (2)	To turn the boat into the wind so that the sails start to collapse
Luffing (1)	Easing the sails so that they are no longer completely filled
Luffing (2)	Turning the boat into the wind so that the sails are no longer completely filled
Lull	A temporary drop in the wind
Median position	The point on a jib track which serves as a reference point for all other jib car positions
New	A term used to distinguish sheets on one side of the boat from the other. As you tack or jibe, the new sheet will become the working sheet after the tack or jibe. The old sheet is the working sheet before the tack or jibe. Can also be used to refer to the wind before and after a wind shift
Old	(see New)
Open	Typically referring to the top of the jib's leech and meaning that the sail has twist.
Point	A term used to say how far away from the wind you're sailing. "Pointing well" means sailing as close to the wind as we can whilst not losing speed
Point (2)	A demand such as "please point down a bit", meaning please steer away from the wind a little
Pointing down	Steering further away from the wind
Pointing up	Steering closer to the wind
Pole	A pole used to hold a headsail (jib, genoa) or spinnaker out from the boat, i.e. a whisker pole or a spinnaker pole

Port	The left hand side of the boat as you look forward towards the front (bow) of the boat
Rudder	The submerged part of the steering assembly
Running	Sailing with the wind almost or actually behind you
Sail	One of the following: headsail (either jib or genoa), mainsail or spinnaker
Sheet	A rope connected to a sail used for trim. This is our primary control rope for the jib.
Sheet on	The action of tightening or trimming-on the jib sheet
Sheet out	The action of loosening of easing the jib sheet
Shift	When the wind changes direction
Shrouds	The wires either side of the mast that hold the mast in place and control its overall shape.
Spreaders	The struts or spars that stick out from the mast and connect to the shrouds to hold the mast up and to control rig tension
Spreader tips	The outboard most part of the spreaders where they connect to the shrouds
Stern	The back of a boat's hull
Starboard	The right hand side of the boat as you look forward towards the front (bow) of the boat
Tack (1)	The front and bottom corner of the sail which is attached to the boat
Tack (2)	The current tack you're on, i.e. starboard tack (wind coming over the starboard side) or port tack (wind coming from the port side)
Tack (3)	See Tacking
Tacking	Changing course by steering the boat through the wind when the wind is in front of the boat
Telltale	The light-weight thread or wool attached to the sails used to visualize the wind's presence around a sail. If they are different colors, then the red one is the port telltale and the green one is starboard
Tiller	The handle connected to the rudder used to steer the boat

Trim	The overall state of a sail, i.e. how it's set by its sheet and other controls such as the halyard or jib car
Trim	To sheet on or tighten a rope, typically a sheet
Trimmer	The person whose responsibility it is to control the set of the sail
Trimming	The activity of controlling the set of a sail
Twist	The amount that the top of the leech is angled out from the boat compared to the leech at the bottom of the sail
Up	A term used to indicate something closer to the wind (as opposed to down)
Wheel	The wheel connected to the rudder used to steer the boat
Winch	A drum that is used to make pulling on ropes easier. It's normally operated with a removable winch handle

Index

Airs   *37, 40, 67, **72***
Airfoil   ***9**-12, 59, 72, 74*

Belly   *19, **23**-28, 31-33, 37, 39, 54, 68, 72*
Beating   *56, **71**, 72*
Backing   *44, **45**, 72*
Backstay   *21-23, 31, **72***
Block   *57, **72***
Bow   *44, 45, 58, **72***
Broad reach   *9, 59, **71***

Car   *14, 21, 23, 31-33, 37, 40, 43, 46, 53, 57, 59, 63, 65, **66**, 67, 69, 73*
Cleat   *12, **17**-19, 72*
Clew   *14, 31, 44, 60, **72***
Close hauled   *65, **71***
Cunningham (jib)   *26, 27, 34, 54, **72***

Depth   ***23**, 24, 26, 72*
Downhaul   *60, 61, **73***
Drag   ***8**, 9, 12, 21, 23, 24, 57, 73*

Foot   *14, **31**, 32, 37, 38, 39, 46, 50, 53, 73*
Footing   ***50**, 71, 73*
Forestay   *14, **19**, 23, 25-27, 59, 68, 72*

Genoa   ***15**, 34, 37, 40, 44, 67, 73*
Gears   *44, **46**-50*
Groove   *19, 23, **26**-30, 34, 54, 68, 73*
Gust   *43, **52**, 73*

Halyard   *16, 19, 21, 23, 26-30, 34, 43, 54, 57, **68**, 73*
Head   *7, 14, 58, **73***
Header   *52, **73***
Headsail   ***73***
Heel   *12, 23, **73***
Helmsman   *7, 26-28, 46, 47, 50, 52, 54, 58, 59, 62, 65, **73***

Leech   *14, 31,* **34-40,** *53, 57, 59-61, 63, 65, 73*
Leech telltales   **14**
Lift   **8,** *9, 12, 21-24, 45, 52, 57, 65, 74*
Luff   *14, 19,* **26,** *27, 40, 59, 65, 68, 74*
Luffing   *59,* **74**
Lull   *43, 46,* **52,** *74*

Median   *37,* **65,** *67, 74*

Points of Sail   *71*
Pointing   *47, 52, 71,* **74**
Pole   *59,* **60,** *61, 74*
Port   *71,* **74**

Rudder   *12, 44, 45, 58,* **75**
Running   **59,** *71, 75*

Sheet   *14, 17, 18, 31, 34-37, 40, 43-46, 48, 50-54, 57-60, 62, 65, 67,* **75**
Shift   **75**
Shrouds   *14, 67,* **75**
Spreader   *14, 34, 40,* **64,** *65, 67, 75*
Stern   **75**
Starboard   *71,* **75**

Tack   *14, 31, 43, 44-46, 53, 54, 71,* **75**
Tacking   **44,** *75*
Telltale   *14, 37,* **40,** *41, 46-49, 52, 57-59, 65, 75*
Telltale window   **14**
Tiller   **75**
Twist   **34-37,** *40, 41, 54, 76*

Winch   *12,* **16-**18, *44, 76*